TOKTOK

speaks TOK BOI →

Kokomo — cargo ritual
cargo novelty items success
uns sweatshop

...n as first speaker
...n learns pidgin

Meri Bokis — very refined as
earthy...
garden / greenhou...

possibly nationalistic
but truly ruthlessly
self-serving chodoristic

...i Roe-Tox high
fashion policy free
...as in late Tokugawa
place urban / suburban
mythical Metroplex

...mer samurai
...or student
popular
...my opnity +
...ligion playing
disassemble ...techno-
...alum minutes culture
thru political + speed
...piration a century
...fter clan-type thinking it over
...ture no ...

· Techno — roubots
dérelicts
close to samurai
class
defeated Indians

· U.F.O. overseers
contact to Cong...
...sults, snoops
beset by natural

Prehistoric
nostalgia

...ough
...riival

Ko...
...workers... pranksters

GARY PANTER
COLA MADNES

Cola Madnes
copyright ©1983, 2000 by Gary Panter
essay copyright ©2000 by John Carlin

All rights reserved. No part of this work may be reproduced
whatsoever without permission in writing from the publisher.

Published by Funny Garbage Press
73 Spring St.
New York, New York 10012
www.funnygarbage.com

Printed in Singapore

Library of Congress Cataloging-in-Publication Data

ISBN 0-9701626-0-x

Designed by Peter Girardi and Helene Silverman

All of Gary Panter's works of art contain the tastes of Philip K. Dick, Picasso, Anthony Burgess, comics, far east movies, and the noisy baroque music.
In other words, a beautiful mix juice born from the base of poison and pain.
Furthermore; he creates the

世界
(world)

filled with

独創的
(originality)

and

刺激
(stimulus)

It excels the limit of time and has been inspired from the Japanese "Godzilla." Gary freely walks through the creative world of reality and imagination.

MR. SHIZUO ISHII
President, Overheat Communications, Inc.
Tokyo, Japan

Y PANTER

ved

the characters

YOUNG JIMBO

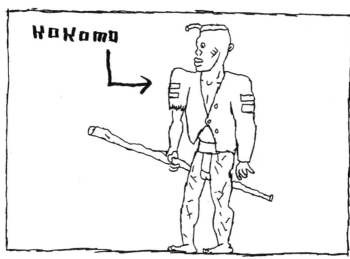

SEP 7 1983

SEP 7 1983

8

BOB WAR

SEP 7 1983

SALARI FUZZ.

9

HENRY WEBB [the Ass-hole]

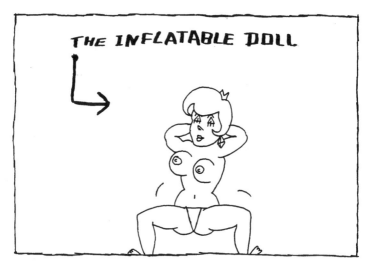

THE INFLATABLE DOLL

MARI BOKIS

SEP 7 1933

THE TREE-MAN [BOKUHITO]

FEB 16 1983

FEB 16 1983

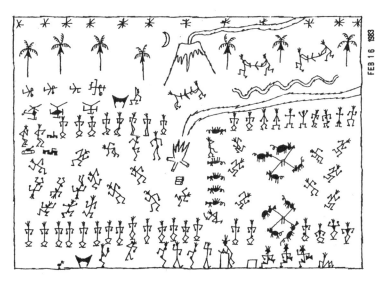

FEB 16 1983

"BOLA MADNESS?"

I'll Tell you something else whippersnapper, you're too smart for your britches. Little brother can get away itcause he's just a kid, but be a m... oh, the door!
KNOCK! KNOCK!!

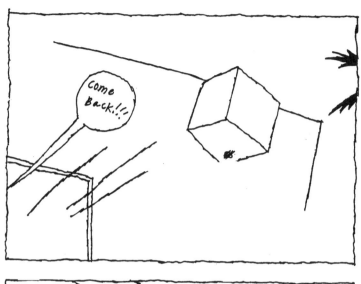

FEB 6 1983

FEB 6 1983

FEB 6 1983

FEB 6 1983

FEB 6 1983

FEB 6 1983

FEB 6 1983

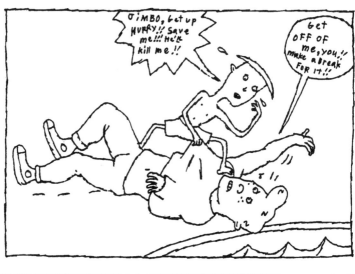

FEB 8 1983

FEB 8 1983

FEB 8 1983

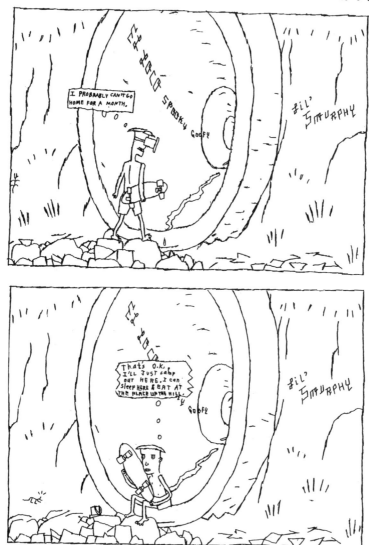

AUG 1 2 1983

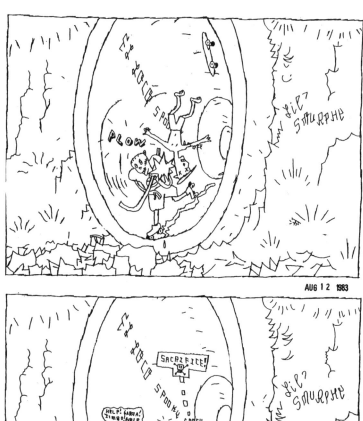

AUG 1 2 1983

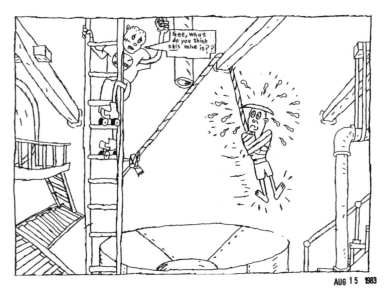

AUG 1 6 1983

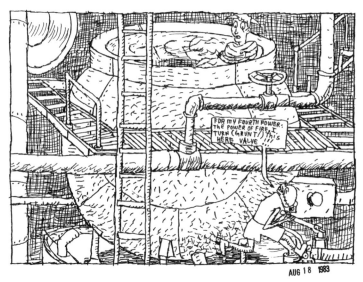

AUG 18 1983

AUG 17 1983

AUG 18 1983

AUG 17 1983

AUG 18 1983

AUG 18 1983

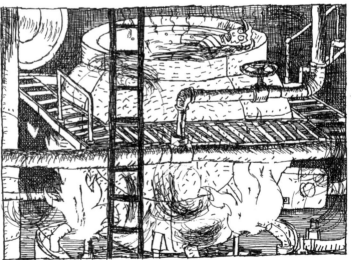

AUG 18 1983

AUG 2 2 1983

AUG 2 2 1983

AUG 2 3 1983

AUG 2 3 1983

AUG 2 4 1983

AUG 2 6 1983

AUG 29 1983

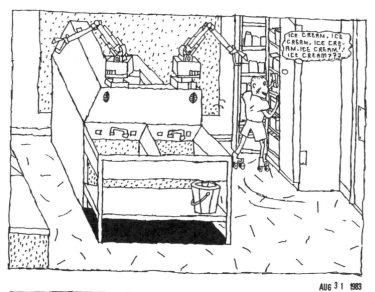

AUG 3 1 1983

103

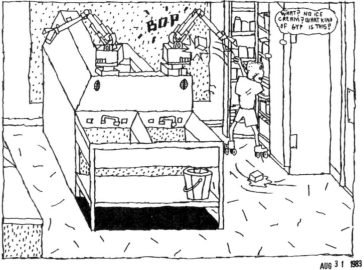

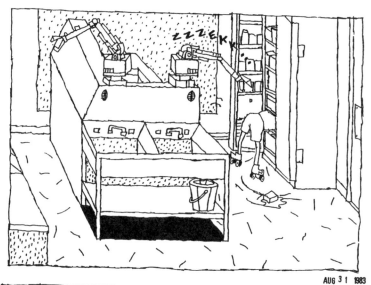

105

AUG 3 0 1983

AUG 3 1 1983

AUG 3 1 1983

111

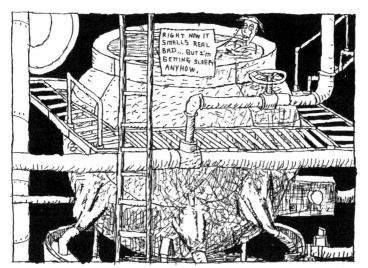

AUG 2 4 1985

AUG 2 5 1983

115

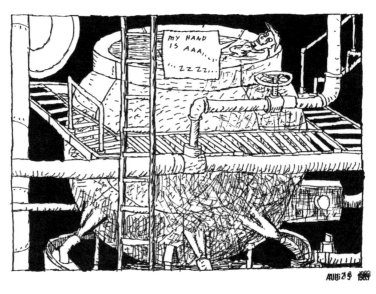

AUG 2 5 1983

AUG 2 9 1983

127

SEP 2 1983

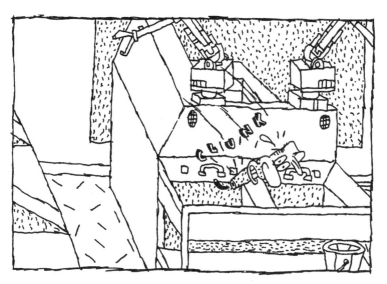

SP/UT

SEP 2 1983

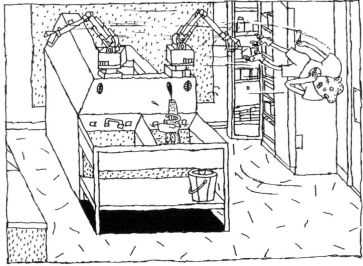

AUG 18 1983

SEP 2 1983

SEP 4 1983

SEP 4 1983

SEP 4 1983

149

152

SEP 5 1983

FEB 19 1983

FEB 19 1983

AUG 2 8 1983

SEP 6 1983

170

SEP 6 1983

175

SEP 6 1983

179

AUG 2 6 1983

AUG 2 7 1983

183

¿Cola, Madres?

CROSSING THE LINE

THE PROFOUND AND THE PROFANE IN GARY PANTER'S COLA MADNES

ESSAY BY JOHN CARLIN

COLA MADNES is the legendary "lost" work by comic master Gary Panter. It was drawn in 1983 during a long burst of energy that began with the birth of the punk everyman "Jimbo" in the pages of *Slash Magazine,* and culminated with the debut of the kiddie TV classic *Pee Wee's Playhouse* designed and partly created by Panter. His Japanese agent, Mr. Shizuo Ishii, had seen Jimbo reprinted in Raw Magazine and asked Panter if it could be published in Japan. Panter interpreted the request to be for a new Jimbo comic and set about creating one for the Japanese audience from notes made in the early '70s while a student at East Texas State. These notes had already been the source of puppet shows Panter performed at school in a band called Ape Week with Ric Heitzman and Jay Cotton. Cola Madness came together in the end of 1983 as the most refined narrative Panter created to date. Unfortunately no Japanese publisher was found and only a novelty notepad with a Cola Madness cover and a few drawings ghosted on blank pages was ever printed. The graphic novel sat for 18 years while Panter went on to create a rich body of work—comics, paintings, sets, illustrations and cartoons —that makes him one of the most important contemporary American artists.

mixing signals

When I first encountered Panter's comics in 1981, just before
he created Cola Madnes, I was struck by the way he seemed to
effortlessly juggle the high and the low, the profound and the
profane. I was impressed by how natural and inevitable this
process seemed in his work. Not the outgrowth of some theory,
but the result of living in America at the end of the 20th century.
I wasn't the only reader who felt that Panter's work resonated
on a deeper level than comics were traditionally meant to serve.

Along the way he gathered peers who struck a similar, if not
identical solution, notably Art Spiegelman and Sue Coe, who
also balanced advanced graphic forms with complex thoughts
about self and society. Yet *Maus* and *Dead Meat* are almost edito-
rial in their use of graphic material to support a theme outside
of themselves. In contrast, Panter's work often seems shapeless
and driven more by the sheer virtuosity of his line than by his
underlying ideas. But Cola Madnes illuminates how Panter
makes of this apparent weakness strength.

The straightforward narrative and layout of Cola Madnes
highlights Panter's central theme: we live in a culture that bor-
rows significantly from the past, but we combine and inhabit
these familiar signposts in a unique and ultimately disturbing
way. Panter seems to be saying that we continue to live with the
symbols and rituals of traditional belief systems but have lost
their sense of spiritual purpose. That is the madness that is Cola.

making myths

Cola Madnes begins with a tribal figure moving silently through
an industrial landscape. He carries buckets, spears, an ax, bow
and arrow. He sits on an abandoned tire and eats a sandwich;
fishes with a net and spear while giant refineries loom in the
background. His clothes shift from tribal skirts to machine-made
shirts without apparent logic. Suddenly he is shown walking

KOKOMO

with a clipboard and pencil, a fedora, briefcase and umbrella.

Then it is nighttime. He sits writing in his bedroom. The moon shines outside. A fan whirls overhead. A voice from beyond calls his name "Kokomo", and invites him to a party being given by John Frum, king of America. Kokomo worries that he is poor and has only one pig to bring to the potlatch, but the voice encourages him, "tonight the world is turning upside-down", and promises that Frum will throw out the boss man and give him chocolates, a jeep and his own plane.

Kokomo and his pig join a procession drawn like Mayan hieroglyphs. As they party and partake in rituals they begin to resemble patterns drawn by the Native Americans that lived on the Great Plains. Finally exhausted, they fall into a deep sleep and Kokomo dreams....

A man with a lizard head and sunglasses named Uncle Garcia goes to get the morning paper. A calendar near the door reads: "8947". Uncle wishes the dinosaur balloons he ordered would come in the mail. He is annoyed that the two boys who live with him aren't up yet. But the younger one, Bob War, is in the next room watching cartoons on TV. He goes and wakes the older boy, Jimbo, by throwing a bomb in his bedroom. "KA BOOM" shakes the house while Bob War sneaks off to play and Jimbo enters grumpy, looking for something to eat.

While Bob War plays outside in the pool with a rubber knife and snorkeling gear, Jimbo and Uncle Garcia bicker about drinking cola for breakfast: "14's too young to get the Cola Madness," Uncle complains, causing Jimbo to mutter: "Cola? Madness? You crazy old people and your crazy old superstitions!!! Cola Madness!!"

There is a knock at the door. Garcia gets up hoping his dinosaurs have arrived while Jimbo goes out to the Jack-in-the-McTaco to get some food. The postman delivers a box. Garcia struggles to open it and slips on Bob War's skate lying around. The box flies off and lands outside in the pool where Bob is snorkeling. Garcia fishes it out only to find an inflatable doll in place of his beloved ancient lizards.

Bob War wanders off to avoid his Uncle's wrath and skateboards into a huge drainage pipe where another boy, the evil Salary Fuzz, skates by with his hockey stick and snares him. Salary tortures Bob in the elaborate sewage plant he occupies. The centerpiece is a huge vat of shit that sits directly under the McTaco.

The Postman, a.k.a. Henry Web, a.k.a. The Asshole is also going to the fast food joint. He sums up his worldview: "I hate everything. Boo hoo." Meanwhile, Jimbo has picked up a little tree man named Bokuhito on the back of his scooter on the way to McTaco. Web is already inside ordering from the kimono-clad waitress Mari Bokis. He lives up to the Asshole moniker and begins to physically harass her while Salary Fuzz skates in to add to general mayhem. Mari beats the crap out of the Asshole while the robotic fast food defense system goes into action. Then Jimbo drops off Bokuhito who wanders in just as things are settling down.

Web and Fuzz sit together in a booth happily eating their tacos. But Web is still feeling ornery and decides to attack the little tree man, not realizing a fierce Godzilla-like monster lurks within.

The tree monster cuts off Web's head, which pirouettes across the restaurant like Garcia's box at the beginning of the story.

While Bokuhito wreaks havoc, Web's headless body kidnaps Mari and drags her to his car. All this escapes Jimbo who sits outside happily eating his morning taco and cola by the drivethru.

There is a terrible climactic explosion as the tree man grows to dwarf the scene. He picks up Web's car and throws it through space knocking into everything in its path, including Jimbo. At that moment Kokomo peers into his own dream.

In the next frame Jimbo lands in the pool back at his house where Garcia and the Doll are about to get together. Jimbo goes off with the Doll himself, while Garcia goes to look for Bob War. He has freed himself and jumps Fuzz when he returns to the cesspool.

As they struggle, the Asshole's head plops through the sewage pipe and lands between them. His last words end the dialogue: "sad to spend my last moments on earth floatin' in a vat of shit. Well…if it's worth anything, I think I was a much better person this time around…"

Kokomo wakes up, rubs his eyes, looks around and sees a helicopter and some soldiers on the ridge. He runs after them looking for what he had been promised. One speculates, "maybe we did the ritual wrong." Another counters, "No! We did a big fine ritual. Maybe some among us were faithless." Kokomo defends himself as they grab him against his will and carry him to the helicopter to "fly to heaven & lead the ancestors back to our rescue." "A holy mission." Kokomo flies off the ridge in the chopper as the story ends.

a thousand heroes with the same face

This story is presented in a relatively conventional layout. Two uniform panels per page, broken every now and then by a two page spread to provide dramatic emphasis and show off the graphic skill that gives the quirky plot such resonance.

The choice of form was the product of two sources. First, Panter's mistaken understanding that the book was being created for the Japanese market. In his mind it was a story imagining what America might be to someone Japanese. So the form resembles standard popular Japanese graphic novels gobbled up by commuters. Second, the book grew out of notes made in the 1970s

for puppet plays that Panter put on in art school and collected in notebooks titled *Terrapan, etc.* In this sense the standard panels are a proscenium through which the action on stage can be seen.

The puppet show plays itself out as an alternating series of sequences that introduce characters, propel them into action and then bump them into other characters. This is a convention that goes back at least as far as classic Greek drama. Here it is more like Oedipus Wrecks. There are no fathers—only uncles and assholes surrounded by sullen aimless kids; no moms—only dolls. I think this apparent mix-up is not only on purpose, but also historically significant. Panter apes the expected forms of drama and graphic novels only to fill them with content that deliberately disturbs and confuses.

Panter's notebooks prove the method behind this madness. Each character evolved from exhaustive experimentation. For example, a page from Terrapan shows Kokomo evolving from two distinct sources: a typical anthropological caveman and Fred Flintstone, a cartoon caveman. Here we see, literally, how two popular icons (one from TV, the other from natural history) are synthesized. This exercise not only illuminates how the character developed stylistically, but also the deeper theme at play throughout Panter's work: how everything we can imagine is a crude patchwork of junk posing as reality. But the remarkable result of this equation in Cola Madnes is not post-modern irony, but a sort of pre-modern symbolic resonance. Kokomo is not a gloss on Fred Flintstone, but an affectionate rejection of its superficial universe in favor of something deeper and more ambitious. An attempt to reinvest the cheap consumer culture we live in with genuine spiritual significance.

In fact, the controlled point of view and graphic design in Cola Madnes contrasts sharply with most of Panter's comics in which the line and enveloping frames are heavily manipulated as part of the overall development of the work. For instance, in his current and most ambitious Jimbo comic, a version of Dante's *Purgatory*, each page can be seen either as a series of panels telling a story or as an overall pattern that is greater than the tale itself. In fact, during the time Cola Madnes was drawn, Panter's work was typically experimental and expressionistic in its use not only of framing devices, but also stylistic shifts within the work. These ranged from conventional ink lines to thick washes and gestures typically associated with painting rather than comics.

Consequently, Cola Madnes' conventional form yields an unparalleled emphasis upon the action, character development and the mix of symbolic elements in the landscape. Above all, these experiments highlight Panter's ability to indicate mass through line—a more difficult task than one might imagine. His characters appear as more than cartoons. They are neither ironic nor iconic. They are complex creatures who inhabit a world that has been thought through to the last detail. The notebooks prove this. Backdrops are not decorative embellishments, but pieces of whole worlds that Panter brings into being even as he controls our view of them like an old master.

In this regard Cola Madnes is part of traditional American storytelling that has survived in vernacular genres such as science fiction, westerns, mystery and comics rather than in literature or fine art. Perhaps the most obvious parallel is with Panter's so-called cyberpunk peers such as William Gibson and Rudy Rucker who also owe much of their science fiction to the work of Philip K. Dick. Dick was among the first to understand that American culture at mid-century was changing more than anyone wanted to admit. Along with more intellectually celebrated peers such as J.G. Ballard and William Burroughs, he pioneered a type of fiction in which drama resulted from the

TERRAPAN

progress of a central character through a world that seemed ordered and rational on the surface but whose center did not hold.

Most of the great artistic achievements of American culture have touched upon this theme. And in this way various degraded genres like science fiction, rock'n'roll, horror and the western join the comics in offering an unlikely medium for the expression of truths not allowed in mainstream art or culture.

I did not understand this for a long time. I could not see how artists like John Ford and Alfred Hitchcock related to R. Crumb or the Beatles. But now I do. Moreover, I understand how the western could inspire Japanese films such as Kurosawa's *Yojimbo*, which in turn influenced and improved the evolution of the western in Hollywood. And how, finally, how the spirit of the western could be reborn as science fiction in work such as *Star Wars*, *Neuromancer* or *Jimbo*.

I used to hate westerns, having grown up in the post-hippie era. Associated John Wayne with Ronald Reagan and jingoistic simplistic sentiment. Thought of John Ford as a sentimental hack responsible for perpetuating the slaughter of native Americans. But I was wrong. Looking at the work as an adult, and not how the work has been misunderstood culturally, I realize it is the resonant American myth. Not the triumph of the individual hero over the odds or the god given destiny of Europeans to dominate native Americans and ultimately nature itself; but the unresolved duality that exists within the individual and nature. Ford established the myth of the Western only to use it to set deeper timeless themes about the fundamental disjunction between self and society. That the connection between each and all is not a transcendent spiritual abstraction, but the opposite —the flux itself. The Searchers are just that. The Mess is the Message after all.

Resonant within Cola Madnes is this struggle with American

themes, which has also at its root universal human themes. Panter's genius is to allow these elements to exist in process through his work without resolving them. The central theme of Cola Madnes is the movement of simple characters through mad synthetic sign systems. A world of accretion that is testament to what humans have left out, not what they have achieved. The most obvious example of this is that the fulcrum of the entire story is a fast food restaurant located on top of a sewage treatment plant (a ribald joke on the human digestive system.) These pilgrims of evil and desire orbit around this empty edifice only to be blown to bits by... a nature symbol out of control. The little tree man, Bokuhito is the key to how it all unravels. Cute little twiggy nature one moment, then the tempest. This implicit duality anchors the entire story from the mix of pastoral and industrial in Kokomo's landscape to the way in which the story doubles back onto itself. This deliberate bringing together and holding apart two separate strands is what takes Panter's comic story into another realm altogether.

Panter's work not only plays upon this deep strain where American art and entertainment meet, but also advances it further into a mass culture where rootlessness is both fundamental and fundamentally obscured.

the line that drew the world

It is remarkable how little has been written about the ability of a few people to create complex characters and stories with line drawings in a series of frames. It is a sad mistake that this legacy of the 20th century has been relegated to marginal status. Recently the Whitney Museum of American Art presented a year- long, immense survey of American art and culture with thousands of objects culled from painting, film, music, design, sculpture, photography, etc. to represent "The American Cen-

Physical
splashes

Garcia
Blows
her up
then
Converse

Johnny's in the Pool
Fighting a Donald
Duck Float
inflatable girl

Rear Projected
L.A. silhouette

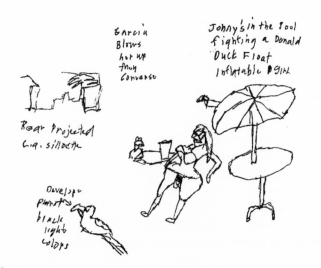

Develope
photos in
black
light
colors

tury." Not a single comic strip made it into the show. And yet I am not the only one who has found comics to be one of the greatest forms of expression in this century—and the repository of the best drawing and graphic design to be found anywhere. This is part of what makes it so difficult to place Panter into art history. His peers in the late '70s and early '80s, from Keith Haring to Mike Kelly, made it into the museums by adapting the presentation of their work to an accepted gallery context, even while seeming to subvert that context. But Panter stuck stubbornly to truly obscure and degraded forms like notebooks, comics, album covers and TV sets. He never got the form of accepted artistic expression, but he sure did get the fundamental basis for art—he made lots and lots of drawings. More than anyone else. And as a result he raised the level of his craft beyond approach.

Like most gifted artists, Panter was born with it. His early drawings show precocious talent. His father ran a five and dime store in Texas and made traditional western paintings on the side. By the time he was in high school Panter was a local legend for his drawing ability. He went to art school and began exploding the drawings across a variety of media, then went to L.A. to seek his fortune just as the Punk Rock scene was about to begin. Panter's scratchy, seemingly untrained line became as much a symbol of the era as fuzzy three chord loud songs. Jimbo emerged at that time in the pages of *Slash Magazine*, the epitome of L.A. Punk attitude. Panter also began doing work for Frank Zappa and the Residents' Ralph Records that deepened his connection to the underground music scene. Just as R. Crumb's funky old-timey lines became the symbol of hippie culture, Panter's raw designs summed up the do it yourself aesthetic of Punk.

When that style became omnipresent, Panter reinvented his public persona and anticipated the new wave scene through his groundbreaking designs for a performance artist named Paul Reubens who called himself PeeWee Herman. This launched another wave of imitators and by the end of the '80s one couldn't turn on a TV set or open a magazine without seeing Panter's acidic candy colored influence upon pop culture.

Rather than capitalize on his own successful styles, Panter began concentrating on the more personally focused work that had been the root of his popularity. This manifested itself in the series of Jimbo comics that appeared in *Raw Magazine* and were reprinted, with new additional material, in the early '90s. Panter also began a series of large-scale paintings that he showed in New York after moving east in 1987. The paintings were largely derived from notebook drawings, but dramatically changed the scale of the line and added unexpected uses of color ranging from graceful canvas soaked stains to harsh surface blends in which the pretty seemed to threaten and undermine itself.

Throughout this remarkable history the center of Panter's work remains the line and his unmatched skill at drawing things in a way that appears utterly simple but impossible to duplicate. Cola Madnes presents a unique sustained example of his work at the crossroads between a young artist struggling to find his voice and a mature one obsessively looking for forms in which to express it.

The source of the Cola Madnes style is the same unlikely mix of traditional comic books and pop art painting that fuels most of Panter's work. This particular book seems like the bastard offspring of Jack Kirby and David Hockney, both of whose work, in turn, is an amalgam of 19th century illustration and 20th century pop culture.

Kirby's influence can be seen in the layout, particularly the simplification of forms in the service of plot, the sense of physical mass in the relation of characters and backgrounds and the occasional cubistic breakdown of expected forms into explosive force fields to punctuate and pace action.

Hockney's influence is seen in the feathery lightness of the line, the graceful relation of lines to each other abstracted from theme and the use of negative space to focus each composition in support of the narrative flow.

Other influences abound, particularly the use of grotesque that began with Bud Fisher (*Mutt and Jeff*) and E.C. Segar (*Popeye*) and resonated in underground comix; the use of tonal contrast and complex points of view that cartoonists such as Milt Caniff and Harvey Kurtzman share with filmmakers such as Hitchcock and Ford; and the startling jumps in logic that gave George Herriman's *Krazy Kat* such a remarkable artistic character. (Don't forget that Krazy Kat's surreal antics took place in Coconino County, surely a significant factor in the name of Cola Madnes' dream weaver, Kokomo.) In many ways Cola Madnes is a controlled compendium of influences, graphic and thematic, that make up Panter's universe.

And yet, like most great artists, Panter is able to take these borrowed threads and make something unique and original from them. However one can trace influences upon Cola Madnes, in the end it is totally unique and unlike anything else in the history of comics or graphic illustration. In fact, this book, lost and forgotten for almost twenty years, represents the beginning of Panter's mature career. This is where he put it all together and began drawing one of the most remarkable bodies of work any American artist can claim. All in the profound guise of profane characters circling the banal. That is the genius that is Cola.

BOB WAR AND JOEY   LIVE IN the SAME
It IS Never SAID AS to whether they are frater
though generally it will be assumed. Their li
is full of adventure And tension.

JIMBO AND NANCY LIVE IN ANother Rea
the realm of work ritual and MAINtenance rit
They do have an affection And lust for each
They want to be alone   , They get tired
, bored, so do the child

The children are exper
already are well programe
diversionary institutions
lack of insight, attenti

Though the life Jim
of leisure they are pr
activities then begin c
vie for their time,
quiet satisfaction)

PAUL lives in the
student of   Information is his fa
and friend. At various times he attaches
himself to objects around the house, trea
them as conscious entities ! Especially math